CAESAR

My Special Wild Mustang

Booklocker.com, Inc.
2007

CAESAR

My Special Wild Mustang

HWA-JA RACHEL MARKS

CAESAR
My Special Wild Mustang

Grief

Adoption
Trust
Friendship with Ruby
Schmoozing with Buck
Playing with Big Red
Exploring Together
Mesquite Beans
Jogging along
Moonlight Outing
Water Boy
Saddle Up
Road Trip
Teaching and Learning

Week 1 - 2
Week 3 - 4
Week 5 - 6
Week 7 - 8
Week 9

The Day After
Farewell

Hwa-Ja Rachel Marks

GRIEF

Grief is a relative emotion.

Some people may not give any thought when they hear about someone losing a pet or may think it is silly to grieve over a pet's death. I might have been one of these people until I watched Caesar put to rest.

If you love your pet so much that you cannot imagine being apart from each other or if you have experienced grief over the death of a pet whom you loved and cared for, this is a story about my Caesar that I would like to share with you.

Caesar was more than just a horse for me. He was the best friend I could have had among any horses. Caesar was shy, gentle, and playful and taught me so much about how to be a good friend and how to show love and caring.

Caesar was born in May, 2003, and was put to rest on May 20, 2007, after being treated for nine weeks. Unless I was out of town, Caesar and I spent every day doing something together since we adopted him on February 28, 2004. Those three years, two months, and three weeks were good times we had together.

Caesar will be in my heart forever.

ADOPTION

When we went to Apache Junction where the Bureau of Land Management (BLM) held a one day affair for people to adopt wild mustangs and burros, we didn't intend to adopt any horses since we already had three at home. When we saw a small colt with a beautiful flaxen mane spread on both sides of his neck, we changed our minds and decided to adopt him.

When the silent auction was about to end, we noticed that a young couple was also interested in the small yearling palomino. The silent auction started at $125 with $5 increments and more than a sheet of paper was used between us and the young couple. At the end, a BLM officer changed it to a verbal process to save time. I was not about to give up in spite of the fact that he had a terribly soiled tail because of bad diarrhea. Needless to say, he was the highest priced yearling mustang adopted that day.

Since we went there just to look, we didn't have any way to bring Caesar home. We found someone in the neighborhood who had a four-horse trailer and was willing to travel five hours round trip. Caesar came home with Ruby whom we also adopted.

Ruby is a strawberry roan mustang and I wanted to name her Strawberry, but settled for Ruby due to my husband's objection to Strawberry. Come to think of it, that seems to be one of his rare objections. During our over 22 years of marriage at the time, I was so accustomed to "whatever you want" from him.

We put Ruby and Caesar together away from the other three horses so they could get accustomed to us and their new home. I noticed Caesar's big eyes that reminded me of a scared young child hiding behind his mother. Even though Ruby was a month younger, Caesar was smaller and always hid behind Ruby when I approached. I would say, "Hey, you are a boy. Grow up to be as brave as an emperor Caesar."

My husband said that Caesar would always hide behind Ruby unless we separated them. With a panel fence through the center of the round pen, Caesar was near Ruby, but was not able to hide behind her anymore. At feeding time, I would walk through Caesar's area to put Ruby's hay in her feeder, put Caesar's hay in his feeder, and sit on a plastic chair near his feeder. Caesar would step up, grab a mouthful of hay, and retreat to chew. He repeated this until he finished his hay while I was sitting there. After one week, Caesar decided that he could eat his hay without 'grab and retreat'. I just sat there watching him eating hay for another few days.

A BLM officer told us that grass hay for a couple of weeks would clear his diarrhea, but it didn't help. Dragging a twelve-foot lead rope that we were supposed to leave on his halter until he was tamed, Caesar looked awfully dirty and it was hard to tell that he was a palomino with a beautiful flaxen tail. Per our vet's suggestion, I tried Pepto-Bismol and various diarrhea pills crushed in his feeder with little hay flakes when he was hungry. It seemed to help only temporarily and I ended up using all methods known to treat human diarrhea, including non-fat yogurt, for over a year with little success. During this experimentation, I found out that Caesar really liked bananas.

TRUST

We know that trust is an essence of human relationship. A friendship or business relationship without trust would not last very long. I learned that establishing trust was the first step before Caesar would let me near him.

During the first week, when Caesar saw me sitting there behind his feeder, he ate his hay with a 'grab and retreat' routine before deciding to stay at his feeder and eat. It took more than an hour for Caesar to finish the hay while I just sat there in a plastic chair. Apparently, my husband saw me doing this day after day from his home office window. A couple of weeks later, he said, "I didn't know that you have that much patience." Well, I didn't know it either.

Something about Caesar developed my patience. I sat in the chair for at least three hours a day until Caesar felt comfortable taking hay from my hand. Once Caesar trusted me to feed him, he would lick hay flakes from my hand or any lingering banana flavor from my fingers.

Ruby, who was separated from Caesar only by a panel fence, decided that she could trust me also. When she approached the fence after she was done with her hay, I grabbed a little hay from Caesar's feeder and let her take it from my hand. To my surprise, when I was outside of their round pen, Ruby came and stood sideways next to the fence as if to say, "Touch me." I reached in and touched her side and back and she stood there enjoying the contact. Encouraged by Ruby's behavior, I reached in for Caesar and found he was not quite ready for it. Apparently, it was one thing to eat off my hand and it was another to let me touch him.

After they were done with their morning hay, I walked across the round pen, through the inside gate between them and slowly approached Ruby to touch her side and back. After a few days of repeating this, I picked up Ruby's rope and led her slowly around the pen. I was very aware of Caesar watching us and brushed Ruby gently where Caesar could see us clearly.

After watching me and Ruby for a week or so, Caesar decided to trust me a little more but let me know that he could kick. He kicked out a little to let me know that I needed to be cautious with him. I held a plastic dung fork behind his hind legs when I picked up his rope for the first time. Caesar saw the dung fork and decided to respect me in addition to trusting me. Even after letting me touch his body and following me around when I had his rope, Caesar was still shy with his head and face.

While my husband was in the Phoenix office for a day, I decided to move Caesar and Ruby to the corral where the other three horses were. Considering that they were not quite tamed wild horses who spent less than a month with us, I was taking a risk. I knew what could happen if they decided not to follow me after coming outside the round pen, but I was determined to move them while my husband was away.

After setting up an area for them to go inside the corral gate without any interference from the other horses, I proceeded with Ruby and then with Caesar. When Caesar saw a white storage shed near the corral, he stopped and would not move. Oh, no. Now what? Caesar, please trust me for twenty feet more. Please. I gave him a hay cube from my pocket to relax him and take his mind off the shed. I had heard that chewing would relax a horse and it worked. Caesar chewed on a hay cube and moved a couple of steps. Chewed on another hay cube and moved a few more steps. Chewed on another hay cube and moved more steps. Soon we were inside the corral. When my husband came home, I was just finishing up with rearranging the panels to give the young ones a bigger space away from the corral gate.

Caesar and Ruby were busy investigating their new surroundings and smelling the other horses that came near the panel fence. It was time for them to get to know and learn to trust the other horses. I was just happy that Ruby and Caesar trusted me enough to follow me from their round pen to the corral 500 feet away.

FRIENDSHIP WITH RUBY

Traveling together in a strange trailer for almost three hours creates a special bond between two horses. No doubt, both were scared to be forced into a trailer by BLM officers and to find another unfamiliar horse dragging a twelve-foot lead rope. I can only imagine how scared I would be if I was locked in a small moving trailer with a stranger. Soon after Caesar and Ruby were unloaded from the trailer into the round pen prepared just for them, I noticed that Caesar and Ruby were walking around closely together checking out the new place. When one stopped, the other stopped and they stood closely together.

After giving them some time to get familiar with their new home, we slid a feeder and a water tub under the panel fence. They stood for a while and walked closely together to the feeder and ate hay looking at us often while we stood outside the round pen watching them. When Ruby was ready to drink water, Caesar would follow her and they drank together.

The next morning, I walked in with an armful of hay and noticed that Caesar would move behind Ruby with his big eyes peeking at me. After I left the round pen, they walked to the feeder together. This pattern continued for a few days until we managed to separate them by putting a panel fence through the middle of the round pen. They could still smell each other, stand close to each other, and share water from the forty gallon water tub under the panel fence between them.

On the second day, Sunday afternoon, we happened to catch them taking a nap. Ruby was sitting down and Caesar was lying down on his side with his hind legs on Ruby's back. Ruby didn't seem to mind it at all.

She was one month younger than Caesar, but was already acting as an older sister looking after Caesar. Until we put the fence between them, they always stood together, napped together, and rested together looking at each other.

After I moved them to the corral where the other horses were, their closeness continued. When my husband hung one feeder on the fence and installed one automatic water dispenser, I noticed Caesar and Ruby standing head to head, happy to share hay and water, not fighting even once. They still look so cute together in several pictures I took while they were eating hay and drinking water.

Even after we removed the fence and allowed them to mingle with the older horses, Caesar and Ruby still hung around together, napped together, and groomed each other. Caesar and Ruby had a special friendship.

Later when Caesar was in his own area during his illness, many times I found Ruby standing alongside Caesar only separated by the panel fence.

Ruby lost her grooming and napping buddy. I feel bad for Ruby whenever I see her standing there all by herself. When I get a chance to brush Ruby's neck, Ruby actually tries to groom me back on my shirt. I cannot imagine how much she misses Caesar. After Caesar was gone, Ruby kept looking for Caesar for a long, long time. My tears well up again when I see Ruby looking around for Caesar after each bite of hay.

SCHMOOZING WITH BUCK

We adopted Buck and Big Red a year before adopting Caesar and Ruby. When Buck and Big Red came home together, we put Buck in the corral with Shadow and put Big Red in the corner of the corral alone separated by a panel fence because Big Red was a yearling who was not tamed yet and would have been harassed by the older horses. Buck was a large four year old gelding and assumed his leader role immediately over Shadow, a seven year old Arabian gelding. It was interesting to see how quickly Buck took his place as boss as soon as he looked around his new home. Shadow went back to his previous owner two years later, and I still can see Shadow's demeanor whenever Buck looked at him. Buck displayed a presence that matched his big body and his wild mustang heritage.

When Caesar and Ruby moved into the corral, Buck smelled them and let them know that he was the boss even though there was a panel fence between them.

After a couple of months, when I was able to take Caesar's halter off and on without any trouble, I led Caesar and Ruby out of their protected area to see the other horse's reactions. Shadow, Big Red, and Buck seemed to accept them fine. They were not really strangers since they had interacted over the panel fence for two months.

I let Ruby walk around with her halter on and led Caesar. Caesar stood close to me and acted comfortable when I was between him and Buck. I literally told Buck to be nice to Caesar as Buck smelled Caesar. It could be my imagination but Buck acted as if he understood my command and responded to Caesar when Caesar smelled him back. I walked Caesar close to Buck several times a day for a week or so. When they greeted each other with friendly nose touching, I removed the fence that separated Caesar and Ruby from the older horses.

Caesar knew that Buck was the boss. Any time the other horses started to bother him, Caesar went to Buck for protection. I saw Caesar schmoozing with Buck and Buck accepted Caesar as his small buddy, worthy of his protection.

No wonder that Buck misses Caesar so much. Between Ruby and Buck, I wonder who misses Caesar more. While eating hay or hay cubes, Buck looks around for Caesar. He even stops eating and goes near the fence looking over the hill where I used to take Caesar for a walk. Even though we do not speak the same language, I understand how Buck feels. What a friendship they can share with each other.

I saw Buck's attitude change toward Ruby. Buck used to be merciless toward Ruby before Caesar was gone and Ruby did not dare go near Buck unless she wanted to be chased and bitten by him. Both Ruby and Buck miss Caesar a lot and Buck is much nicer to Ruby. Buck lets Ruby come near him now and even lets her eat next to him once in a while. Ruby does not seem to be so afraid of Buck anymore and follows Buck around right behind his tail. I wonder what brought about these changes. Is it possible that missing Caesar's presence brings them closer somehow?

PLAYING WITH BIG RED

When we adopted Buck and Big Red in 2003, Big Red was already a big boy as a yearling. We put him in a corner of the corral separated from Shadow and Buck in his own area about twenty feet square.

During the trip home, I read every page of 'Wild Horse 101', a booklet that was given to us by the BLM. Soon after we unloaded Buck and Big Red, based on the little knowledge I had from the booklet, I went inside Big Red's pen, walked around slowly far away from him, and came out slowly. I was very scared. After all, this was my very first contact with a wild mustang. When I went inside the third time, Big Red approached me before I had a chance to get out. "Brendon, what do I do?" I yelled out quietly. "Stand still and touch him gently." Big Red was already taller than I was but approached me with his head low and I was able to touch his poll gently while trying to hide my fear.

He was so trusting and seemed to enjoy my touch. This was not the wild horse I read about in the booklet. He seemed to be so friendly and trusting, which I thought was very baby-like. So, I suggested 'Baby Red', but my husband reminded me that he won't be a baby horse too long. We decided to call him Big Red based on his size and color.

I was so thrilled when I brushed Big Red all over the first time within a week. Wow, I was way ahead of what the little booklet described in taming a wild horse. Maybe, Big Red is such a trusting horse that anyone can tame him easily. Nonetheless, I was excited when we removed the panel fence between the horses only a couple of weeks later.

It was Big Red who made me think it was fun to tame wild horses. My husband was working in Phoenix and I was up here in our county home alone during the week. I had lots of time to play with Big Red every day. But things changed a year later when we adopted Caesar and Ruby. My attention was switched to the little ones and Big Red hardly saw me other than at feeding time.

After moving Caesar and Ruby into the corral, Big Red saw me coming to the corral more often, but still didn't get to spend time with me. I was busy paying attention to Caesar most of time. I didn't notice how Big Red was acting up.

One day, I went into the corral, passing by the other horses and through the small gate into the area where Caesar and Ruby were. Big Red was right behind me when I closed the gate. I shoved him off to close the gate and spoke to Caesar who came to me. I heard a crashing noise from the panel fence behind me. "What are you doing, Big Red?" I yelled and noticed blood dripping from his mouth. Apparently, he held the panel fence in his mouth, lifted it up, and dropped it because I didn't pay attention to him and shoved him away to close the gate.

I didn't know that a horse could get jealous for affection. Our vet had to pull two teeth and put several stitches in his gums. For two weeks, Big Red was on a soft food diet with hay cubes soaked overnight in water. After this episode, I paid more attention to the other horses while spending most of my time with Caesar. I learned that feeding alone was not enough for Big Red. They all have different needs, some more than others.

After removing the fence, I observed their behavior mostly out of concern for Caesar. Buck seemed to act as

Caesar's protector even though he had no mercy for Ruby. Ruby did not dare to be near Buck. Shadow used to chase Big Red around, but quickly lost his dominance over Big Red who got bigger in a year. Shadow didn't dare bother Caesar knowing Buck was there for Caesar, but took chances with Ruby. Poor Ruby ended up being chased by all three older horses, but she moved fast to get away from them most of time. Caesar was the only one safe for Ruby. After all, Ruby was the big sister who looked after Caesar from day one.

Big Red knew that Buck was Caesar's protector, but tried to get to him anyway. Caesar learned quickly that it was better to play with Big Red than to try to get away from him. They played head to head or nipped each others hind legs. Big Red is a big boy over sixteen hands and Caesar was barely fourteen hands. To Big Red, playing head to head meant just raising his head, but to Caesar, it was a different story. Caesar had to stand on his hind legs as tall as he could. It was something to watch. Caesar somehow managed to meet Big Red mouth to mouth and did not give up. Most of the time, Big Red had enough and walked away but Caesar would still chase after him. I wish I was quick enough to snap their pictures while they were playing head to head.

Caesar schmoozed with Buck who was his protector, played with Big Red to have fun, and befriended Ruby whom he shared meals with, groomed with, and spent his resting time with. Caesar never fought with anybody and knew how to get along with each horse in a different way.

I realize now that horses may not understand the death of a friend or grief over death. They just know that a friend is not there with them any longer. Ruby, who used to stand next to Caesar at dinner time, still stands in her spot, leaves Caesar's space, and looks around for him. When I let her out of the corral, she smells Caesar in our orchard, goes around the mesquite tree under which Caesar is buried, looks over toward next door where she used to follow us, and nickers for him. Buck, who used to look after Caesar, keeps looking over the street and the hills for Caesar even during dinner time. On the other hand, Big Red does not seem to miss Caesar and is always happy to get something to eat.

I see each horse reacts differently to Caesar's absence as we grieve in different ways. Some people may think that I cry too much for Caesar, but I doubt that my tears will dry up for Caesar any time soon. I am glad that I have my husband around me who understands how I feel about Caesar.

EXPLORING TOGETHER

We live next to a creek and our property is surrounded by hills. It is about a mile on a lightly-traveled dirt road from our small rural neighborhood to the paved road. It is quite a nice setting for walking. Even though I don't care much about walking, I enjoyed walking with Caesar.

When Caesar was safe enough to be outside of the corral, I took him out for a walk. We walked just a short distance in the beginning and would hide under mesquite trees on the uphill slope across the road from our property. I would sit under a tree and let him eat grass or mesquite beans. Neighbors passing by hardly noticed us there. Caesar was such a small yearling that he fit just fine under a tree. We spent many days of Caesar's first summer under mesquite trees.

As he grew older, he grew stronger, but slowly in size. I didn't want to put too much weight on him with a saddle but wanted him to get familiar with the surrounding hills and roads where we might go riding someday. As the hot summer days were winding down, we started walking farther and farther. We walked across the creek, over the hills, down to the paved road and turned around to head back home. Sometimes, our walk took over two hours and I was too exhausted to walk back home, especially when we were walking up hills. I stood behind him holding his lead rope in one hand and his tail in the other. Caesar would turn his head, look at me, and walk back home pulling me slowly. I was never afraid of being behind him knowing that he would never do anything to hurt me.

I walked many places with Caesar where I would never walk alone. Walking over an hour to the edge of the hills and looking down at the creek below was quite an experience. Caesar was so careful with his steps that I never had to worry about our safety.

When we had long walks, I carried a bottle of water in one pocket and Caesar's treats in another. When we stopped for a break that I needed, I drank water and let him have a sip from my hand. Whenever I drank, Caesar knew that he would get a treat from me. Whether it was a banana, carrot, or mesquite beans, it didn't make any difference.

We walked together on the dirt road so many times that our neighbors driving by started to notice us. As long as I was next to him, Caesar walked with me or stood by me quietly. Our neighbors all knew what a good boy Caesar was. After a while, our neighbor, Jim, told me that Caesar was welcome on his property any time. Jim had the best grass in the neighborhood during the winter.

Caesar was the best walking buddy I ever had. Actually, the only walking buddy I have had.

MESQUITE BEANS

Caesar and I walked everywhere in the neighborhood hills. During our walks in late spring, we took notice of which mesquite trees might have more beans later in the summer. Then, when the mesquite beans were ready, we stopped at trees which had lots of beans first and saved trees with less beans until later. Caesar could reach beans on small trees, but waited for me to pick beans for him most of time. Less work for him and more work for me. Neither of us minded a bit.

During our walk to find a good mesquite tree, if I saw a nice patch of grass, I let Caesar graze for a while. If he missed a good spot, I squatted down. If I happened to spot a good tree, I reached up for mesquite beans. As soon as Caesar saw me squatting down or reaching up, he walked over to me. Caesar knew that I found something good for him to eat.

I got carried away once and we walked over two miles away from home looking for better beans. Crossing to the other side of the creek, we found trees loaded with beans and Caesar had a great time eating enough beans for his lunch. It was a long walk back home and I decided to go back the other way to shorten the distance a little bit. After putting as many beans as possible in my pants and shirt pockets, we passed by the only gas station in town and crossed a narrow bridge. Even though this was his first time walking on a bridge, Caesar walked quietly alongside me. I was so nervous every time cars passed by on the bridge, but Caesar did just fine. As soon as we were on the paved road past the bridge, I pulled Caesar over on the dirt to calm myself. Caesar stood there with me just watching cars go by. After about a half mile walk on the paved road, we came to the dirt road that led to home. We stopped several times on the way, emptying one pocket each time.

After we arrived home, I kept thinking about how many beans we left behind on trees and decided to train Caesar to carry beans back home. I put saddle bags over soft towels on Caesar's back for a few days for him to get used to walking with saddle bags hanging down on his sides. Then, we started the journey to collect those beans with one bottle of water and two carrots in each saddle bag. On the way to collect beans, we finished one bottle of water and two carrots. When we got to the trees, I picked beans telling Caesar, "One for you, one for them" until we filled up both bags.

When we walked on the bridge this time, I was not nervous knowing Caesar would be just fine. We stopped several times on the way home because I needed to rest. I drank the other bottle of water and Caesar finished the last two carrots and some more beans. It was after we got home when I realized what a heavy load Caesar was carrying. I could hardly lift the saddle bags off his back. Afterwards, I decided to stay closer to home when collecting beans.

Oh, I know. For Caesar, it was not work. It was fun for him to walk around with me and to eat mesquite beans at every tree we stopped at even if he was carrying saddle bags. And Caesar got his special treat every time we arrived back home: an extra banana, apple, or a carrot and my praises. He liked to hear "Good boy, Caesar" while eating his treat.

JOGGING ALONG

I like running or jogging even less than walking. I ran in a race only once over eleven years ago. To celebrate my 50th birthday, or not to make the 'big five-oh' bother me, I decided to run in the Phoenix 10K. Of course, 10K is a heck of a lot farther than a mile and I needed help from my husband who used to run regularly. We purchased our property twelve years ago and we were coming up here for weekends from the Phoenix area. From our property to the paved road is about 1.2 miles of winding up and down dirt road. My husband thought that this road would be a good place to prepare me for the Phoenix 10K.

My husband prepared me well for the race and I finished the race with him running alongside me. I did quite well considering it was my first race. To be honest, I had some help to finish the race. When I was getting too tired to maintain my pace, I saw people passing me by who motivated me: a lady who was twice my size, a little boy who was not quite tall enough to reach my waist, and an old man over 80 years old. I could not have finished the race as well without their help.

Anyway, after Caesar and I walked enough around the neighborhood, I was thinking that I might want to run the same race again when I turn sixty. Some people run in a race every week, every month, or every year. I thought it would be cool to run once every ten years. I didn't want to ask my husband to be my trainer again and was thinking if I could train myself on the same dirt road, I would make it just fine.

When I walked on the dirt road with Caesar, I told Caesar, "Hey, you could be my running training buddy." When I was ready to jog, I held Caesar's rope in my hand and started to run slowly saying, "One, two, one, two." Caesar didn't know what I wanted him to do at first, but soon caught on. It took only a few tries before he started to trot every time I said, "One, two, one, two." When Caesar's trot changed to a canter and I could not keep up, I stopped running and he stopped with me. Soon, Caesar learned to trot and canter very slowly to match my speed. He moved with the rhythm of my voice, "Good boy, Caesar, one, two, one, two, Good boy, Caesar."

This new trick for Caesar to run with me came in handy when we had to cross a busy street. When we walked down to the paved road, there were always cars passing by. I had to wait for a gap in the traffic before running across the street with Caesar. All I had to do was say, "One, two, one, two." I told Caesar that there were better grass or mesquite beans across the busy street. Truth is that I wanted to show off what a good team we were. I believe Caesar was proud when he heard, "Good boy, Caesar, we did it!"

MOONLIGHT OUTING

Stars seem to shine much brighter in the country and the moon seems to give more light on a country road. You can see well at night for many days around the full moon. I would go out around 10 pm while my husband was getting ready for bed. There is some advantage for me not to have to go to work. I could stay up as late as I wanted and spend some time with Caesar in the moonlight.

Even though Caesar was my favorite, I still had to be fair to the other horses. Usually, I had carrots, apples, or bananas enough for all of them. After everybody got to eat their treats, I would open the gate a couple of inches. Caesar would notice a little gap in the gate and walk slowly to me as if when he walked slowly, the other horses would not notice him moving. When he got to the gate, I opened it a couple of feet more and he would sneak out. By the time the other horses got to the gate, Caesar was already out and the gate was closed. I didn't use a halter or a rope on Caesar. He would walk with me or a little ways from me. It didn't matter either way. I let him enjoy himself for a while. I knew Caesar would know when it was time to go back to the corral.

Some people told me that Caesar was spoiled. Both Caesar and I knew that he was spoiled, but it didn't matter to us. He enjoyed being spoiled and I enjoyed spoiling him. After working in the round pen, walking up on the hill and jogging along on the way home, or after a ride, I used to take him to the front door of the house or to the stairs in the back and tell him, "Wait, Caesar." After a few times, Caesar learned that I would be back with a treat and waited for me.

One day I took Caesar to the front door and went upstairs to get his banana after telling him to wait. As I was heading to the kitchen for his banana, the phone rang and I was on the phone for a while. Sometimes, I forget what I started to do after getting distracted with something else. This time, I got distracted with the phone call, forgot all about Caesar's banana, and went about my business until my husband came inside and told me that Caesar was still at the front door. Caesar was happy to get an extra banana which was my way of saying, "Sorry, Caesar. I didn't mean to forget you."

After his special treat at the end of a moonlight outing, Caesar would follow me to the corral. Once in a while, he would turn his head away from the gate telling me he was not ready to go back in. When this happened, I held his face between my hands saying, "Caesar, it's time to go in." Then, I would remove my hands from his face and point to the gate saying, "In, Caesar." It is still amazing to me how well he understood it. I never had to use a halter or a rope on him for our moonlight outing. It was always fun for me and I believe it was fun for Caesar too.

Now when the moon shines bright, I cannot bear to go out to the corral. I take care of Ruby, Big Red, and Buck as I should, but I don't know when I will be able to go out in the moonlight again. Time heals everything, as they say. I doubt that time will make me miss Caesar less, especially when the moon is high and bright.

WATER BOY

We don't know any other horse who likes water as much as Caesar did.

When we watch a horse training program on RFD-TV, if the trainer starts to talk about teaching a horse to get used to a small amount of water first before taking the horse to cross a creek, my husband and I look at each other smiling. For sure, we don't need to train our horses with water. None of our horses is afraid of the creek. Actually, our horses like to go in the creek every chance they get.

We have a creek that runs along the west side of our property with a fence along the other three sides. We didn't fence the creek side because a fence too close to the creek is torn out at each spring runoff and a fence too far from the creek wastes the lush creek-side forage the horses could eat. I thought that they would stay on the property as long as we kept the gate closed at the end of the driveway.

I don't like to keep our horses cooped up in the corral all the time. Even though the corral is big enough for them to run, they just walk and stand around most of time. I like to let them out of the corral so that they can graze wherever they like. I especially like to see them running around the property. For whatever reason, one horse would start to run, the rest would follow until they circle the property several times, along the creek side, around the guest house, behind the house, and then into the orchard. We call one area 'the orchard' even though all we have there are three big mesquite trees and three small apple trees that survived the Texas root rot that killed most of the thirty-seven apple trees planted with my husband's sweat. When there were plenty of spring grass or mesquite beans on the property, I don't have to worry about looking for them. My husband warned me many times that horses were horses and they would not stay on the property unless it was completely fenced. Soon, I found out that he was right.

Caesar was the first one who proved me wrong. We were sitting on the swing on the east deck watching the horses enjoying themselves. After a while, I noticed that Caesar was not in sight. I went around all three sides of the deck calling him. After many times of yelling, "Caesar, where are you?" Caesar showed up and looked up where I was standing as if to say, "I am right here." He was dripping water all over from his small body and we knew that he had been in the creek. We were laughing hard and wondered how fast he ran when he heard me calling.

Caesar knew that I was looking for him anytime he heard "Caesar, where are you?" Many times after the incident, I had to look for him. Sometimes, he was on the other side of creek amongst the plentiful grass and weeds. Other times, he was in the middle of the creek just having a good time, pawing and splashing water.

When he was the only one away, all I had to do was yell, "Caesar, where are you?" Once in a while, he would look at me and continue to eat. When I knew that he had seen me, I would walk away from the creek still yelling, "Caesar, where are you?" Quite often, Caesar ran out of the creek so fast that he was at the corral gate long before me as if to say, "Are you looking for me? I am right here." Sometimes, he took his time getting out of the creek, knowing that he could not get to the gate without me seeing him, he would run and slow down to walk to me. Caesar was clever enough to know when to run to the corral gate and when to walk to me.

Obviously, he was my favorite and I let him out on the property more than the others. My theory was that if he was the only one out, he would not get in trouble as much. Time after time, he proved me wrong and I ended up using several towels drying him off. My husband pointed out that it was not necessary to dry him off, but I didn't want him to catch cold especially after sundown during the winter. I would start with his face first and then down his back, belly, legs, and tail. Caesar acted as if he was enjoying all the attention and stood still when I waved towels drying him off. After doing this enough times with many towels, I didn't let him out late in the day. If he got all wet when the sun was high, I didn't need to worry about him catching cold.

To be fair to the other horses, I could not let Caesar out alone all the time and left the corral gate open once in a while for all of them to have fun roaming around on the property. Even though I was inside the house, I knew that they were in the creek when I heard the loud splashing sound of water. Apparently, Caesar showed them the way to the creek. Whenever I happened to see them heading to the creek, Caesar was in the lead. Even after I saw them, I left them alone thinking that they would come home eventually.

One day, they didn't come home even after sunset. Usually, they would sample the grass and weeds across the creek, get in the creek playing in the water with each other, run upstream, and end up in the neighbor's field eating more grass. I knew their routine since I had to go and get them from the neighbor's property many times. I would only take Buck's halter which has a twelve-foot lead rope. When I found them, I put the halter on Buck, put the other end of the rope around Caesar's neck, and walked home between them. They knew it was time to go home and didn't give me any hassle. Big Red and Ruby usually followed us home.

This particular afternoon, I got busy doing something in the house and didn't go out looking for them before sundown. It was getting dark and we went out to the same area looking for them with a flashlight. We could not find them anywhere and I was worried that they went downstream and got lost. My husband assured me that either they would come home during the night or we would find them in the morning. There was no moonlight. How could they find their way home?

My husband got up at dawn and drove to the top of the hill to see if they were anywhere nearby. Since they didn't go upstream as usual and would not go downstream because it was unknown territory with rough terrain, he thought that they would be most likely somewhere on the other side of the creek.

The neighbor on the other side creek has a huge property of about 260 acres. After searching for them through his binoculars, my husband came home and woke me up. Apparently, the neighbor across the creek had left his gate open and our horses walked into a meadow and they didn't miss their hay. Brendon said that they looked like they were heading back home. We crossed the creek and met them, but when they saw us, they turned the other way. I called Caesar while squatting down, remembering what we used to do when we were out exploring the hills, and Caesar came to me. As soon as we crossed the creek, they ran right into the corral. Even with so much they ate all night, they still went for hay in the feeder.

This happened only once but once was enough. Whenever they disappeared from the creek, I was able to find them on our neighbors' property upstream. My husband keeps telling me not to let them out of the corral, but I still do. I just cannot stand to see them confined in the corral all day long.

When the weather gets too hot for me to walk over to get them upstream, I let just one of them out. When the other horses are in the corral, one horse outside the corral stays on the property.

However, I couldn't guarantee that Caesar would stay on the property when I let him out alone. He would usually sneak out to the creek to play in the water and to eat grass on the other side. When I heard the splashing sounds from the creek, I knew that Caesar sneaked out to the creek again, but didn't worry. I let him stay there for a while to enjoy himself. I knew that Caesar would come back home when I called him, "Caesar, where are you?"

SADDLE UP

After watching Clinton Anderson's 'Round Penning Made Easy' and 'Riding with Confidence' training tapes several times, I started to train Caesar after my husband set up a training round pen for us.

We started with changing direction in the round pen and then moved on to the lunging stage. Soon, I was able to lunge Caesar outside of the round pen. All I had to do was point one direction and then the other direction. Following Clinton's training tape instruction worked out just fine for us. After I was able to get on and off Caesar's bare back using a step stool, I started to sit on his back using the panel fence while he was eating hay. Caesar didn't seem to care how long I sat on his back.

After Caesar was used to my weight, it was time to try the saddle. I did all the desensitizing exercises with him and he was now three years old. Even though my saddle was a light-weight saddle made with synthetic material, I was not able to carry it from the garage to the round pen. I either had to keep the saddle in the round pen or introduce the saddle to Caesar in the garage. In the Arizona sun, keeping the saddle in the open area would ruin it quickly. Caesar needed to get used to the garage.

To have Caesar get used to the garage, I lured him in with a snack. After a few times, Caesar would follow me into the garage, without a halter, expecting a snack. When he got used to the garage, I tried the saddle blanket on and off and then the saddle. When Caesar got excited, I settled him down with "Good boy, Caesar." Even though I had his halter on him, I didn't have to use the rope to hold him still most of the time. Once in a while, when he moved backward a couple of steps, I tugged the rope gently and he moved forward the same number of steps. It didn't take long for Caesar to stand still when I put the saddle on him in the garage.

I had him get used to the saddle by walking and lunging him around the round pen for a few days before I mounted. While he was getting used to the saddle, Caesar never reacted badly, not once thinking about bucking. Knowing how calm he was with the saddle on, I also stayed calm when I mounted.

After my husband built a hay shed next to the corral, he moved an old aluminum storage shed that used to hold hay behind the new hay shed to store saddles, bridles, halters, and all other related items. It worked great for me to saddle Caesar after my husband added another gate so that I could let Caesar out of the corral to stand next to the storage shed.

There was enough room for Caesar to turn around and walk through a passageway between the new hay shed and the corral. This small area was exclusively for Caesar. Due to Caesar's condition that persisted since the day we adopted him, I was always looking for ways to treat his diarrhea. I used this small area to give him different snacks or feed every day while the other horses were eating hay cubes for lunch.

This small area was a special place for Caesar to get his treat every day. I had no problem to saddle Caesar here. He would stand without being tied while I would clean him, brush him, and put on the saddle blanket, extra gel pad, and the saddle. My neighbor could not believe that I could saddle him without even a halter. Caesar was gentle and cooperative with the whole process. When the saddle was snug enough for him, I put the halter on him, put fly repellent roll-on around his eyes, and tugged his rope gently for him to turn around.

Caesar's bridle is a combination style with a halter that made it easy for me. After a simple exercise routine in the round pen, I snapped the hackamore attachment to the halter. When the hackamore was attached, Caesar knew that it was time for me to mount. Not like my previous horse Shadow who was always on edge, Caesar stood calmly for me to mount. I was always anxious when I got on Shadow, but was never nervous to get on Caesar.

I always felt safe with Caesar not only during the mounting, but also during the ride. I am a novice rider and all I could do before Caesar was hang on the saddle horn while a horse was walking. Even though I was following Clinton's training tape to train Caesar to ride, I always felt safe with him.

I would not have dreamt to trot with any horse before Caesar. Caesar made me feel that I could try to trot. After a while, I got enough courage to trot in the round pen and then out on our property. I remember how great I felt when we trotted on the dirt road outside of our property. We walked on the hills and crossed the creek after I gained enough courage to trot on the road. As if he knew that I was nervous about trotting away from home, Caesar trotted nice and easy and helped me build confidence. We walked a little longer to an open area of the hill and trotted for a while. It is hard to describe how Caesar helped me to be brave.

Caesar knew that I didn't want him to eat while I was on the saddle. Once, when I let him walk around in an open field, he walked to a strange place next to a barbed wire fence and stood still. "What are you doing, Caesar?" Then, I realized that he stopped there because of tall weeds. He could nibble on them without putting his head down. Apparently, Caesar figured that as long as he didn't put his head down, he could nibble a little. I gently reminded him with, "Caesar, no eating while I am on the saddle."

After that incident, I usually dismounted and removed his bridle after a long ride and let him graze for a while before heading home. The combination of halter and bridle worked out great for this too. Chewing with the bridle on would not have been comfortable for him.

I am so grateful to have had time with Caesar for the last three years. He was the only wild mustang that I tamed, trained, and rode. And I am the only person who ever rode him. Caesar was so careful with his steps that I never worried about us getting hurt when we were out on the hillsides. He taught me to ride and trot with confidence. Caesar was the most gentle wild mustang friend I could ever have known.

ROAD TRIP

When Caesar was doing well with his training in the round pen, we acquired a used two-horse trailer. We were thinking about taking Caesar and Buck on a road trip someday, possibly camping on our 36-acre property in northeast Arizona.

Caesar was just over two and still small. He was not ready to climb on the trailer two feet above the ground. My husband built us a platform a foot above ground that was four feet wide and eight feet long. I led Caesar up to the platform that led right to the trailer until he was comfortable to get on and off the platform. Only then, Caesar was ready to try the trailer.

After several tries of 'front feet in and back out', Caesar finally walked up into the trailer. Once he was in the trailer and backed out, he seemed to enjoy getting on the platform and into the trailer. After a couple of weeks, we removed the platform and Caesar had no problem stepping into the trailer. After a while, all I had to do was say, "In, Caesar." Of course, Caesar got a treat every time after he got off the trailer when I gently wiggled his tail.

After Caesar turned three and was comfortable loading and unloading from the trailer, I signed us up for a Western and English riding class at the community college. Not that I was so much interested in learning to ride better, but wanted Caesar to get to know other horses. Occasionally, he ran into neighbor's horses across the creek, but Caesar was too shy to get to know them. I figured that it would be good for Caesar to actually spend time with other horses.

The class was held about thirty miles away from our home at the instructor's place. I didn't want Caesar to travel that far as his first time in the trailer. The fall semester was still more than a couple of months away and we had some time to have Caesar get used to the trailer trip. We started out with a half mile trip and expanded to a mile and then two mile trips. Caesar seemed to be doing fine so far.

By the time Caesar had a few short trailer rides, Buck was ready to go in the trailer with Caesar. We took both of them out for a trailer joy ride a few miles away from home. I called it a joy ride because both of them got to be out of the trailer and had time to graze for a while before coming back home in the trailer. We walked around with them until we could find good places for them to graze. It was fun for us to watch them enjoying themselves. Sometimes, we found lots of mesquite beans for them to eat, and brought some home for Ruby and Big Red.

After many short trips in the trailer, I thought that Caesar was ready for the class trip. Since I was not able to drive the truck hauling a trailer, my husband had to go to the class with us. When Caesar got in the trailer for the first day of class, I put in enough snacks for him to nibble on during the trip.

When we arrived at the class location and opened the trailer front door to let him know that he would be off the trailer soon, I noticed that Caesar was quite anxious. When he came out of the trailer, I led Caesar to eat some good-looking grass. Caesar was not interested in eating and was breathing hard. I didn't know that a horse could hyperventilate.

I rubbed his neck telling him, "It's OK, Caesar." many times. It was a while before he calmed down and we walked around slowly until he was breathing normal. I didn't realize what a strange place after a long trailer ride could do to him.

We were the first one there and had a chance to walk around in the arena. When the class began and I mounted, the instructor on another horse wanted to lead Caesar by a long rope. That horse was much bigger than Caesar and was a stranger to Caesar, and Caesar reluctantly followed them. I think that I was more nervous than Caesar was because I didn't know how Caesar would react to all this. We did all right for the first ten minutes and then Caesar relaxed enough to follow the other horse closely. Caesar finished our first class just fine. I was so proud of us when a student complimented how nice Caesar trotted.

On the way home, we stopped a couple of places and checked on Caesar to find Caesar much more relaxed. Caesar didn't have any problem when we went to the second class. He actually walked closer to the other horses and even passed other horses at a trot.

I regret that we didn't have a chance to travel to our 36-acre property and let Caesar run freely enjoying himself and grazing there. I can almost see him running around and having a good time on the wide open place.

TEACHING AND LEARNING

I am not sure if I taught Caesar more or I learned more from him.

The taming process was lengthy because Caesar was such a shy boy. It took much longer for him than the other mustangs. During the long twelve-week process until I was able to easily take his halter off and on, Caesar slowly learned to trust me. Once I earned his trust, everything else was a matter of practice. For me, it was time to learn more about being patient.

I have seldom had any patience with anything. Being such an impatient person by nature, it was amazing how patient I was with Caesar. I would sit on a chair morning, noon and evening until he finished his meal. March is still a cold month where we live and I would bundle up in a heavy coat and sit there to let Caesar know that I was there to take care of him and it was OK to trust me. After five to six weeks passed by, I felt like it was taking too long to tame a mustang, but never lost my patience with Caesar. Something about Caesar, who still had diarrhea even though I was doing everything to help him, made me try harder and do more for him. I was amazed that I was buying expensive organic fat free yogurt for Caesar when I would never buy it for myself.

Day after day, week after week, my husband watched me spending time with Caesar during this long taming process. He finally told me that if I could practice a little of that patience with him, it would be nice. To this day, I am quite patient with the other horses we have, after learning to be patient with Caesar.

Caesar learned to trust me and I learned to trust him too. After taking him out to walk many times, I learned to trust Caesar to walk with me without a halter. He would follow me around as if he knew what I wanted. In the round pen, when I got courage enough to try trotting, I trusted him to go at my speed. I was so excited when Caesar trotted a couple of circles carrying me nicely. I would have never tried trotting with any other horse. Caesar was gentle and carried me well during the trot.

After a few more sessions of riding Caesar at a trot, I was ready to leave the round pen. I managed to open the gate and told Caesar to stand still while I counted numbers out loud. It was mainly to calm myself but also to teach Caesar to stay in the round pen until I was ready. I remember counting numbers one to twenty very slowly. Caesar didn't move as if he was waiting for me to be ready. When I was ready, he walked out of the round pen slowly. Caesar was very patient, which made me feel safe

Caesar taught me not to be afraid to try a few different things on horseback. I wonder if I would ever feel safe again with any other horse as I did with Caesar. I know that I trusted Caesar as much as he trusted me. This was a beautiful experience for me. The bond we had between us was a very special one.

WEEK 1 - 2

It was a nice Sunday afternoon in late March and I remembered that our neighbor Jim's place was the only place that had a nice patch of green grass during cold days. Jim told me a couple of years ago, "Your colt is welcome here anytime," after seeing Caesar and me walking up on the hills many times. Jim was impressed how well Caesar behaved every time he saw us walking together.

We have only three neighbors: Jerry and Esther on the south side, Dave on the north side, and then Jim on the north side of Dave. Our neighbors all knew that I took Caesar out to walk with me quite often and we had their permission to enter their property any time.

It was a good day to take Caesar to Jim's for an afternoon snack. We walked over to Jim's and I found the patch of green grass still looking good. Caesar seemed to be interested in the patch in the beginning, but was not eating the grass as he normally would. "Caesar, what's matter? You liked the grass here before. Do you want to try something different?"

After watching him for a while, I took him home. I didn't know why he was not interested in eating the grass but thought that I would treat him with his favorite snack. I was stunned when Caesar would not eat the banana. "What's the matter, Caesar? Are you sick?"

I never had an opportunity to take a horse's temperature before, but Caesar stood still for me. The thermometer registered 106, but I didn't know what their normal temperature was. I took Buck's so that I could compare it with Caesar's. Buck's was 101. Caesar definitely had a fever. I stayed with him during dinner time to see if he would eat hay. Caesar seemed to nibble away slowly standing next to Ruby.

Over the years, we had to make three emergency calls to a vet. Once when Shadow had colic and twice when Big Red injured himself. Shadow's colic was over by the time the doctor got here, but he gave me a tube of Banamine Paste to use if it happened again. Big Red needed quite a few stitches on his neck once after running into a barbed wire fence and then a second time to fix his gum injury. We didn't have any knowledge about fever or Bute. I so regret that I didn't make an emergency call or didn't have Bute paste to lower Caesar's fever. My husband says that it would not have made any difference. Based on what happened for the next nine weeks, he may be right, but I still regret that I didn't make the call on Sunday afternoon.

I called the vet's office when I woke up Monday morning. They asked me to take Caesar's temperature again. It was 107. A doctor and an assistant came within an hour. She gave Caesar a Bute injection and had me wet Caesar's feet with running water to lower the fever. I now know that high fever could damage their internal organs and any temperature over 102 should be treated.

She wanted to give Caesar an IV liquid treatment, but was not able to find his jugular vein to insert a catheter tube and decided to give him a gallon of water through a tube into his stomach through his nose. I felt so bad for Caesar to go through this ordeal but was proud of him for tolerating all the needle pokes for half an hour while the doctor was trying to find his vein. The doctor said that his skin was as tough as an elephant and his vein location was unusual.

The doctor's examination showed that Caesar's respiration rate was much higher than normal due to his fever and his mucous membranes were red. Caesar's heart rate and lungs seemed to be normal. Not knowing what caused his fever, the doctor took Caesar's blood for a CBC/Chemical panel and left me a tube of Bute paste to give 2g by mouth twice daily until Caesar's temperature went below 100.8. I gave 2g of Bute to Caesar the next morning and his fever went down to normal and he started to eat the neighbor's grass and drank water when I took him to the creek, even though I didn't see him drinking any water at home.

Caesar's doctor was concerned that Caesar would get dehydrated and came to check on him again Wednesday. Monday's blood test showed no bacterial infection, but very high white cell counts. She suspected that it was some kind of virus infection and wanted to do another blood test to see if anything changed. A brief exam showed that Caesar's temperature was down to 100 with normal heart rate and lung sounds.

This time, she was able to insert a catheter tube and sedated Caesar so that we could administer twenty liters of fluid therapy. My husband hung the bags high on the corral roof beam so that the fluid would run steadily. After the doctor left, I sat on a plastic chair talking to Caesar while my husband watched the fluid's steady run. I was grateful that we had light out there and Caesar seemed to be all right standing there in front of me. It took an hour and a half to finish the first ten liters of fluid. I never thought I'd be so glad to see a horse pee. When the first ten liters were almost gone, Caesar stood there and peed as the doctor told us he would. When my husband changed the bags to do the second ten liters, it did not go as expected. We thought we did something wrong when we changed the bags. We were able to give him only two liters of the ten.

When Caesar's doctor came out the next day to check on Caesar's catheter tube, we found out it got kinked when Caesar moved his neck when his sedation started to wear off. She inserted another catheter tube and sedated Caesar again so that we could finish the second ten liters we could not do the night before.

Caesar's fever was up again even with the fluid therapy and I gave him 2g of Bute, which seemed to bring the fever down. At the end of the next day on Friday, Caesar's doctor stopped by and showed me how to give Caesar 15 ml of Baytril through the IV. Caesar's temperature stayed normal for two straight days and I was beginning to think that the Baytril was helping him. But after the third injection, I had to give him 2g of Bute again for fever. Caesar's frustrated doctor told me to continue with the Baytril injection for the rest of the seven days but I had to stop after the 4th injection on Monday because Caesar decided to remove his catheter tube. He was a good boy to keep it in for 5 days. I was told to check on Caesar's temperature daily and administer 2g of Bute if he had fever over 102. Caesar, who really did not like getting the Bute by mouth, had to get it three more times on Tuesday, Friday, and Saturday.

Caesar's doctor stopped by again on Friday to check on him. The exam results were mostly in the normal range except his fever at 102 and a little fast heart rate of 48. Caesar gave up more tubes of blood for CBC/Plus Fibrinogen, Coggins, and EHV-PCR tests.

During the last two weeks of March, Caesar had blood drawn three times for several tests with no specific results other than high white cell counts indicating he had some kind of infection, two different IV injections, seven doses of Bute to reduce fever, a tube down through his nose with water, catheter tubes inserted twice and sedated twice for twenty liters of fluid treatment. In spite of the effort to find out what was going on with him, Caesar's fever was down only for a day or two after 2g of Bute.

I spent a minimum of 5 - 6 hours of day time with Caesar. Not because of his medication, but because of my concern that Caesar was hardly eating hay or drinking water and I did everything I could think of to encourage him to eat and drink. We put panels inside of the corral to give Caesar a private area to have hay to eat all the time. I cleaned his automatic water dispenser daily to check if he drank water when I was not around. Based on how much hay was untouched and how clean the water dispenser was, I knew that Caesar was hardly eating or drinking.

For these two weeks, Caesar ate neighbor's grass mostly and drank water in the creek. I took Caesar to a different neighbor's each day to give grass a chance to grow back and to a certain spot in the creek where he liked to listen to babbling water coming down between rocks and drink a little. Even though he was not well, Caesar seemed to be happy to be out with me to eat the neighbor's grass and stand in the creek water. I was telling Caesar that I wouldn't mind to take him out two or three times a day for the rest of his life. "Just get well soon, Caesar Boy."

WEEK 3 - 4

Caesar's temperature was normal on Sunday, April 1st but he still didn't seem to care about eating hay. I called Caesar's doctor to find out Friday's blood test result. She mentioned that Caesar's blood showed a high level of acidity, which might encourage bacterial infection, and suggested to feed him Arm & Hammer baking soda. I had enough syringes from the previous week's Baytril IV injections and Saline used to flush the catheter tube before and after Baytril. I asked my husband to go and get Arm & Hammer baking soda, dissolved it well in water, and used several syringes to feed Caesar the solution by mouth.

The next day on Monday, the doctor came to give him a rectal exam, requiring him to be sedated again. While he was sedated, she gave him a gallon of water with baking soda via a tube through his nose. I remembered my mother briefly while watching Caesar and wondered how much she suffered when they fed her through a tube for a few weeks before she died two years earlier. I also remembered my younger sister, who has been a nurse over 35 years, saying, "No tube feeding for me" when she heard about mother's condition. I was just hoping that Caesar was not suffering too much.

At least, Caesar had enough baking soda in his stomach, which should do some good. I knew what I gave him using a syringe was not enough to have much effect.

While sedated, Caesar got another catheter tube inserted for another ten liters of fluid therapy. Before we started the fluid therapy, the doctor gave him an IV injection with 4g of Nexcel and also performed abdoninocentosis after shaving hairs off Caesar's belly, but didn't find any fluid. And another blood test for Valley Fever Titer. Poor Caesar was giving up so much for blood tests while he was not eating hay or drinking much water.

I was shown how to give a muscle injection so that I could give Nexcel to Caesar twice a day for the next six days. Oh, how nervous I was with each injection until I used up two bottles of Nexcel. But Caesar was never nervous or anxious and stood still for me during the shot. Every shot ended with, "That's my good boy, Caesar."

On Tuesday, the day after Caesar got a gallon of water with baking soda, the doctor came again to give him one liter of Saline with 30 mg of HCO (Bi-carbonate) through the catheter tube inserted on Monday. I was supposed to give him another liter the next day but when I came home from an early morning dentist appointment, Caesar had the catheter tube pulled out. So, I just continued with Nexcel injections per doctor's direction.

For a few days, Caesar did not have a fever and I was so hoping that the Nexcel injections were doing the job. It was supposed to take care of many bacterial infections even though we didn't have any idea what caused his fever and loss of appetite.

Monday's blood test for Valley Fever Titer came back negative and the doctor stopped by Thursday to draw Caesar's blood for a Strep Equine Titer test. Certain tests like this one could not be performed locally and had to be shipped to Colorado. We didn't mind the additional shipping charges as much as waiting for the results.

I was checking Caesar's temperature three times a day and was starting to feel good about his Nexcel injections, since he didn't have a fever for almost five days. Thursday's 10pm check crushed my good feeling when Caesar's temperature was up again to 102.4 and I had to give him 2g of Bute. Caesar's fever was down the next day and came back again the following day even though we were continuing with Nexcel injections twice a day. We were not the only ones who were frustrated. Caesar's doctor, who was consulting with the other two doctors in the office and specialists in Phoenix, was so frustrated that I could hear her anxiety over the phone.

On Saturday, I went to pick up three medications that the doctor left at the office. After finishing the last injection of Nexcel, we started Caesar's oral medications with eight tablets of Metronidazole three times a day, five tablets of Tagament/Cimetidine twice daily and 4cc of Probiotic once or twice a day.

The tablets needed to be dissolved in water and then mixed with molasses to make it thicker to help Caesar keep them in. Tagament did not dissolve in water quickly and my husband had to crush the tablets for me. Oh, how Caesar hated to get these medications by mouth but cooperated with me enough that I didn't have to ask for my husband's help. We continued this ordeal three times a day for eight days and Caesar did not have any fever during the time.

During the first two weeks of April, Caesar had two blood tests, one sedation, one rectal exam, one belly fluid exam, one tubing with water and baking soda, one catheter tube for ten liters of fluid therapy and one liter of saline with HCO, twelve Nexcel injections, and eight days of oral medication three times a day. If Caesar could speak, he would have said that he didn't mind the shots but his patience was running real thin for getting medications by mouth three times daily day after day. Caesar, you were such a trooper during this ordeal.

WEEK 5 - 6

Even though neither of us enjoyed the oral medication process three times a day, Caesar didn't have a fever for eight straight days, giving us hope that he would get better soon.

After both oral medications ended, I was to continue with Probiotic once a day for another week. Caesar didn't mind one small syringe with 4 cc of Probiotic after getting so many syringes full of medication three times a day. After a week of Probiotic, I started Tagament for another week to reduce the acid level in Caesar's stomach. Caesar started to grind his teeth more noticeably and his doctor thought that he might have stomach ulcer.

Caesar started to eat hay a little more in the corral, but I was still walking him out to our neighbors' for his favorite grass and then to the creek every day. Once or twice, I let the other three horses out on the property with Caesar and they all disappeared to the creek and I had to go upstream looking for them. Caesar looked and acted his normal self before he got sick when I found them all together eating weeds in the creek upstream. One neighbor across the creek told me that Caesar was kicking up his heels, having a good time with the other horses, and Caesar must have been getting better.

Not having any fever for ten days straight and seeing him happy and strong with the other horses gave us even more hope that Caesar was improving.

On Thursday, April 26th, I was concerned that I hadn't seen any trace of Caesar's stool. Since Caesar had his own area in the corral with two different kinds of hay and several trays of special food, it was easy to monitor his intake and output. I had been checking every day to see how much he ate and how much he digested. On this day, I didn't see any trace of his stool. When I called Caesar's doctor, who hadn't been out to check on Caesar for twenty days, she was concerned that he might have an impaction and would stop by at the end of her scheduled day.

In the mean time, I let the other three horses go to Dave's with Caesar by opening a section of fence we use to get to each other's property. Since Dave was out of town and his gate was closed, I felt safe to let all four horses graze at Dave's. I was with them on Dave's property to keep them out of the septic tank area and saw Caesar pooping a normal stool. Caesar used to have a problem with diarrhea before he got sick, but didn't seem to have the same problem any longer. His doctor said that he could not have diarrhea with all medication he was taking. Anyway, when I saw Caesar pooping, I was relieved, but for some reason I wanted to check it closer. I noticed that some poops seemed to have worms which I had not seen before. As I looked closer, I saw that it was mucus, not worms. I called the doctor again so that she would not waste her trip. When I mentioned that Caesar's stool had mucus, she wanted to come over.

Apparently, it is not a good sign to have mucus on the stool. I was told that Caesar might get worse quickly if the mucus on his stool was not a temporary condition. I went teary and could not respond to her questions for a couple of minutes.

After sedating Caesar, she did a rectal exam, gave him a gallon of water and mineral oil through a tube, and gave an IV injection of Benamine. After the rectal exam, I was told that Caesar did not seem to have any sign of internal damage, but I should continue to check his stool for any more mucus. From that day on, checking his stool for presence of mucus was added to my daily check list.

Caesar had a slight fever the next day on Friday, but the fever dropped quickly when I took him to the creek. As my husband suggested, standing in the creek was a better way to cool him off than hosing his feet. His doctor and I agreed not to give him Bute unless his fever didn't go down after cooling him off in the creek.

On Saturday afternoon, I noticed Caesar's behavior changing. He was agitated, stumbling, and started to bite down on the metal panel fence. I didn't know what to do with his changed behavior, but my husband smacked Caesar's face to get his attention and it seemed to stop him biting on the fence for a while. Saturday 10 pm check on Caesar showed a fever of 101.7 and I gave him 1g of Bute since it was too late to take him to the creek to soak his feet in the water.

During these third and fourth weeks of April, Caesar had a slight fever only a few times, which was an improvement compared to the past four weeks, and he was given 1g of Bute only twice. Fever-wise, Caesar showed an improvement and started to eat and drink more. On the other hand, suddenly his stool showing mucus on April 26th and his behavior change on April 28th were alarming events.

WEEK 7 - 8

Caesar's behavior change worsened on Sunday afternoon and he became aggressive to the point that he would come at me with his ears pinned. My Caesar never acted this way even before the taming process. His stumbling also continued. My goodness! What is happening to him?

Even though it was late on Sunday, I called Caesar's doctor and asked if there was such a thing as mad horse disease. I heard about mad cow disease and didn't know if anything like it could happen to a horse. She didn't know, but called me back after consulting with a specialist in Phoenix to tell me that Caesar might have brain inflammation and I should give him 2g of Bute daily to help his condition.

After one 2g dose of Bute, Caesar's doctor stopped by with her assistant at the end of the day on Monday, April 30th. After more research, she suspected that Caesar might have Western Equine Encephalitis based on all the symptoms Caesar showed the last few weeks. After checking Caesar's damaged gums from biting on the panel for two days, she gave him several cups of Equine Senior mashed in water through a tube, but this time Caesar seemed to be very frightened with the process even though he had a tube down through his nose only a few days ago and twice more before then. The doctor commented that he didn't understand what was going on this time due to his brain inflammation. After a while, both the doctor and the assistant had to hold him while I pumped the liquefied food through the tube. Caesar looked terrified and I felt so sorry for him.

I asked her what was the survival rate for horses that have Western Equine Encephalitis and was told 70/30. Seventy percent is a hopeful rate, which is better than 50/50. Anyway, Caesar's stool no longer showed any mucus. That was a good sign, wasn't it?

She gave him an injection of Dexemethosone (steroid) and left three more days of injections with decreasing doses of 20/15/10 ccs. Caesar's condition seemed to improve with the steroid shots and he started to eat and drink more. I wondered how painful it must be with every mouthful of hay with his damaged gums after biting on the panel fence for two days, but he started to eat more. Sometimes, he liked multi-grain hay better and other times, he preferred the alfalfa hay. It didn't matter to me as long as Caesar was eating hay and I maintained a fresh supply so that he could eat as much as he wanted.

Two days after giving him the first shot of steroid, Caesar's doctor came to draw more blood for four different tests: Western Equine Encephalitis, West Nile, and 2 other reportable diseases. Apparently, Western Equine Encephalitis, that she was suspecting Caesar might have, was a state reportable disease and Arizona State was paying for these blood tests. My husband and I just wanted to know why Caesar was sick so that he could be treated properly. We talked about the possibility of Caesar having one of these diseases, but concluded that even the worst disease would be better than not knowing what ailed him.

So far, all blood tests came back negative and the doctor knew what Caesar didn't have, but had no clue what was going on with Caesar. My husband whose patience level exceeds far more than mine was getting impatient with Caesar's situation. We already decided that we would do whatever we could to help him get better, but did not know what else to do other than following the doctor's directions and caring for Caesar as best as we could.

His temperature stayed within the normal range for the week and Caesar seemed to be his normal self before he got sick. I was thinking, "With steroid shots helping him and eating lots of food, Caesar could get better and stronger soon."

On Friday afternoon, the day after the fourth and last shot of steroid, Caesar started to stumble and be aggressive again. Goodness gracious. "Dear God! Please have mercy on Caesar." I don't know how many times I prayed for Caesar since he got sick. "Please, Father. Have mercy on Caesar's body."

My husband went to the doctor's house Saturday morning on May 5th to pick up five more days of steroid shots for Caesar. I gave him his first day shot of 15 cc steroid and Caesar started to behave better by late afternoon. I had been checking Caesar's vitals including his temperature, heart rate, and four areas of his guts while giving his shots daily with decreasing dose of 15/10/10/5/5 steroid. Even if Caesar had a fever, I was not supposed to give him any Bute while he was getting steroid shots. Caesar's temperature stayed within the normal range until his steroid dose went down to 5 cc. He had a fever over 103 for 2 days, and on Thursday, the day after his last shot of 5 cc steroids, his fever reached to 104. One gram of Bute brought his fever down, but Caesar started to have slight bleeding through his nose.

On Friday, May 11th, Caesar continued to have slight nose bleeding and his nose began to twitch. Caesar's doctor came out and drew more blood for another CBC/Plus Fibrinogen test since May 2nd's blood tests for four reportable diseases all came back negative. His blood test results were the same as eight weeks ago and still showed high white cell counts, but no specific indication of what was wrong with him.

On Saturday, after giving Caesar 1g of Bute to reduce his fever of 102.8, I went to the doctor's house to pick up some different medication. Sulfa tablets dissolved in water by mouth twice a day to help with his infection and a Zylexis shot today, Tuesday, and next Saturday to boost Caesar's immune system. Even though Caesar had a high heart rate of 56 over a week (due to steroid shot, we suspected) and had fever for a few days, he was eating quite well. After two days of Sulfa, Caesar stopped eating hay again. After talking to his doctor, we stopped giving him Sulfa on Sunday afternoon.

On Sunday, May 13th, Caesar started nose twitching and became aggressive again. When I approached him to take his vitals, he actually kicked me. It was not a hard kick but Caesar never kicked anybody before and this alarming behavior change concerned me. What is happening with his brain? How inflamed is his brain? Why can't the doctor help him? So many questions, but no answers.

We had my long time high school friend and her grandson visiting us from Korea since May 7th but I was not able to give them my full attention since caring for Caesar was my highest priority. I had planned to travel to many places with them, but could not leave Caesar sick at home. I was grateful that my husband was willing to take them on the road without me and they understood why I had to stay home. Long distance trips including an over-night trip to Las Vegas would have been more fun for them if I was there, simply because I could communicate in both languages. Even though my husband could not speak Korean and they could not speak English, they managed to communicate essential needs.

During these two weeks while he was on steroids, with a high heart rate most of the time and feverish at times, Caesar enjoyed eating hay and drank lots of water.

Whenever I walked Caesar out to the neighbor's and to the creek, I had Ruby out of the corral without a halter. I walked with Caesar and Ruby followed us. Once in a while, I would take Caesar's rope off, watched him at a distance, and noticed that Ruby was always near by, watching over Caesar. When I brought Caesar home, Ruby followed us. She didn't want to be away from Caesar. When I went to check on Caesar before my bed time, most nights I found Ruby standing next to Caesar only separated by the fence. I was thinking, "How sweet! What a good friend!"

WEEK 9

After stopping the Sulfa tablets, Caesar's appetite improved and his temperature stayed within the normal range. His heart rate was still high at 56 even without steroid shots for a couple days. Alarmed by his behavior changes and continued nose twitching, Caesar's doctor stopped by on Monday, May 14th.

Caesar was sedated again for a couple of head x-rays and an endoscope through his nose. Since nose twitching and bleeding were on the right side, she did the endoscope on the right side first. After twenty minutes or so, she decided it looked clean and proceeded to the left side, but she was not able to maneuver the scope to see it well. After giving Caesar an IV steroid shot, she left me four 5cc steroid injections. When she called me back Monday evening, she wanted to perform the endoscope again inside Caesar's left nose, but when she called Tuesday with the x-ray result, she wanted to take extra x-rays on Caesar's head instead. Two x-rays didn't show any bone destruction and they wanted to see more x-rays.

My friend and her grandson were leaving to San Jose on Friday afternoon and I was going to show them Tucson Saguaro Cactus National Park on Thursday before they left Arizona.

I have a nerve-related condition in my hands that makes it very hard to drive too long. To minimize driving time, I had reserved a two-bedroom suite in Scottsdale for two nights. My plan was to drive to Scottsdale on Wednesday afternoon, travel to Tucson and back on Thursday, show them around Phoenix and see them off at the airport on Friday, and return home to Rimrock late Friday afternoon. I could not ask my husband to do this because they needed detailed explanation about the airport security process so that they would not get lost at the airport before arriving at San Jose where a Korean friend would meet them at the baggage claim.

I showed my husband how to give Caesar a steroid shot at 5pm on Tuesday and listed all the things he needed to do for Caesar while I was gone, including what to do with Caesar for additional x-rays on Wednesday afternoon. I informed the doctor that Brendon would be taking care of Caesar from Wednesday afternoon through Friday afternoon. I was not too concerned about being gone for forty-eight hours or so because Caesar was doing quite well after Monday's steroid shot.

I still didn't like to be away from Caesar for a couple of days, especially during x-rays. Fortunately, Caesar's doctor had a cancellation and stopped by around noon. I really didn't want Caesar sedated again and was able to have him stand still by holding the lead rope in front of him and talking to him constantly. Caesar looked at me straight as if he was listening without moving his head and they were able to take three x-rays.

I called my husband each day to check on Caesar. He had a spreadsheet to record Caesar's vitals three times a day and Caesar's medication times. What a good idea. I had been recording all on a special calendar on the wall so that I could see Caesar's progress at a glance. Using the spreadsheet, I could see two weeks at a glance. Later, I copied my calendar information to spreadsheets to keep Caesar's illness history in one place.

I got back home in time to give Caesar his last 5 cc of steroid shot on Friday. My husband told me that Caesar was agitated Thursday night and he had to use a halter when taking Caesar's vitals. It was still daylight after Caesar's steroid shot and I took him out for a walk to the creek with Ruby following us. I didn't see any agitation in Caesar while I was with him for a couple of hours.

A bottle of 900 ml liquid Sulfapyrimethamine arrived on Thursday, May 17th and after talking to the doctor, my husband had given Caesar a 15 cc dose for two days before I came home. Apparently, Caesar didn't give him any trouble taking the medication by mouth. Nine hundred ml would last for sixty days and Caesar's doctor told me that this medication would work well with steroid. I called her Friday night to let her know what my husband said about Caesar's agitated behavior and what I observed after I got home. I mentioned that this was the first time Caesar's behavior changed during the steroid shots. For the last three times, it was before the steroid shots started or between treatments. Possibly 5 cc was not enough dosage for the third time around; it was a higher dose before this week.

I went out to check on Caesar before my bed time Friday. "Where is my beautiful Caesar?" Caesar liked to hear this whenever I went out to the corral at night. He ate his banana, licking off the last taste and was his normal self when I checked his vitals. His heart rate was slightly down to 52 with no fever and normal gut sounds.

On Saturday, May 19th, to make up for the time I was away, I spent lots of time with Caesar.

When we were out before dinner time, Ruby followed us to the creek. She was always happy to stay with us and usually followed us home. This time, however, after eating with Caesar for a while, Ruby left us at the creek and went home. Caesar was really enjoying eating there, but when he realized that Ruby was gone, he wanted to come home. When we arrived at the gate, he saw Ruby at home and as if he was relieved to see her there, Caesar wanted to move on farther along the road. I let him lead us where he wanted to go. We passed Dave's and Jim's gates and ended up at the edge of the hill. Caesar found something he liked to eat and I was happy to see Caesar enjoying himself. When we came back home, I gave Caesar his last shot of Zylexis as scheduled and told my husband that Caesar seemed to be doing well today and that maybe the liquid combo medication was helping Caesar. We looked at each other with hope.

As usual, before my bed time, I went to check on Caesar's vitals. His temperature was normal and heart rate was down to 48, which is closer to the normal rate of 40. It made me feel even better. His heart rate had been too high for over two weeks while he was on steroids. I had enough carrots for all the horses to share and gave Caesar his banana. It seemed one banana was not enough for him. "I will bring another banana for you in the morning, Caesar. Good night, Caesar Boy!" Oh, how I wish that I had given him another banana that night.

The next morning on Sunday, May 20th, my husband woke me up at 6 am. Something was wrong with Caesar. He was stumbling badly. Two different piles of hay I left for him were not touched and the entire ground area was trampled to a fine dust with no trace of old stools that were there before. There was no sign of his bodily function. I should know. I checked it several times a day.

Apparently, Caesar did not rest and had wandered around aimlessly all night. I put a halter on to steady him but was not able to help. He stumbled against the fence and leaned to steady himself. Briefly, I remembered the conversation I had with my daughter a week earlier. How it progressed before letting her Jess go after they had been together over thirteen years. It took only five days for Jess, but everything that happened and what doctors did for her beloved dog were so similar to what Caesar was going through over two months. When I was talking to my daughter, I was so hoping that it would be a different ending for Caesar.

I asked my husband to call Caesar's doctor, who came before 7 am. How could it change like this over night? Caesar wanted to eat, but didn't know how. He wanted to drink, but didn't know how. He went to where he used to eat hay and stood there putting his nose to the feeder, but didn't know how to open his mouth. His nose touched water, but he didn't know what to do to drink. I cannot imagine how hungry and thirsty he must have been all night.

Oh, dear God! I remembered my daughter Esther's email note after we talked on the phone for a while. Mom, you will know when the time comes. I asked Caesar's doctor, "What would you do if Caesar was your horse?" I somehow knew what her answer was going to be.

Caesar's doctor left us alone in the corral for a long while. Oh, I love you, Caesar. I never knew that I could love a horse this much. She offered to save Caesar's mane and tail for me. I asked Brendon to take our last picture together while I was closing Caesar's eyes. Then, I took one last picture of Caesar.

On cold winter mornings, after finishing his hay, as the sun began to warm the air, Caesar used to lie on his side and stretch his legs to take a nap. Caesar looked as if he was taking a nap.

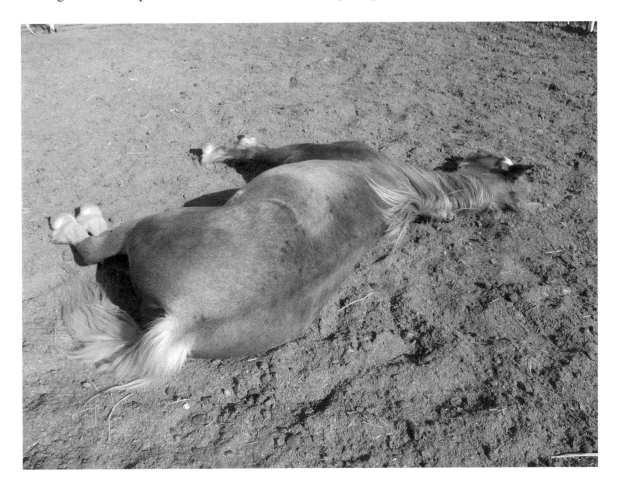

I look at the picture now and he just does not look like he was ill for nine weeks. Caesar does not show any trace of suffering. I suppose it is better for Caesar to go this way than his heart pumping so hard before breaking, due to too much steroid. Maybe, this was better for Caesar, I don't know. All I know is how much I miss him.

The Day After

When I miss him, it feels like every day is the day after we buried Caesar under his favorite mesquite tree.

Our neighbor Jim came over soon after Brendon called him on Sunday morning and Jim worked more than two hours to dig a proper place for Caesar to rest. Apparently, Jim's small backhoe was not equipped to dig hard dirt in a short time. Jerry, a neighbor from across the creek, offered to bring his big backhoe when he realized what was going on, but Jim wanted to finish it himself. Jim knew Caesar because he saw us walking together on the dirt road many times and Caesar had been on Jim's property with me quite often to eat nice winter grass that could not be found elsewhere.

While Jim was working to prepare the place for Caesar, I didn't want any flies to bother Caesar's body. When I touched him to cover certain areas with towels, his stool fell out to the ground. Oh, poor Caesar Boy. He did not know how to poop either.

Neither Brendon nor I had any experience with a death this closely to deal with burying a body. By the time Jim finished digging, Caesar's legs were already too stiff to fold. Jim was nice enough to dig more to lay Caesar the way he was.

Even though I could not bear to see him in the ground, I felt that it should be me to use the first shovel of dirt before Brendon worked with Jim. After all, he was my Caesar Boy, whom I had cared for dearly for the last three years, two months, and three weeks. Brendon had gotten closer to Caesar more this year and I saw Brendon's tears when Caesar fell to the ground. When Brendon held me tight while Jim was putting dirt on Caesar, we both knew how deep my grief was and how many more tears I would be shedding over Caesar's absence. I just didn't realize how much I was going to miss him.

The day after we buried Caesar, we put a fence around the mesquite tree where Caesar was buried to prevent any wild animals from disturbing his grave. We have coyotes, rabbits, deer, and elk walking around at night and wild cats even during the day time. A familiar truck stopped at the gate and it was Caesar's doctor Dusti and her assistant Betty. We were so touched that they cared enough to stop by with a card and flowers. I planted those flowers at Caesar's grave along with a small cactus from the hill across from our property. I used to tell Caesar to be careful not to step on cactus when I was riding him.

When I could not locate Caesar's mane and tail that Dusti was saving for me, I wondered where she could have put them. When Dusti and Betty stopped by, Dusti gave me Caesar's mane and tail braided with blue and white ribbons. They are hanging over a little horse figurine that I bought a couple of years ago while traveling to the Dominican Republic because it was the same color as young Caesar. I never dreamt that I would be using it to hang Caesar's braided mane and tail.

I went through all the digital pictures of Caesar and spent the week to print and organize his pictures into a 3' x 5' picture frame to hang on a wall. I didn't want his image fading from my mind, especially since I have started to forget names and misplace things now at the early age of 61. When I was arranging his twelve best pictures for the frame, I noticed how cute he looked when he was little three years ago when we adopted him. Caesar's color had changed to more grayish on his body and his mane got darker while his tail remained beautiful blond.

After Caesar was buried, I kept wondering out loud how it could change so drastically over night when Caesar was doing so well the day before. Saturday was a good day for Caesar and me to enjoy the weather and each other.

Brendon shared with me then what Jim told him before. Jim's wife, who suffered with cancer, was doing better one day, up and walking around, and Jim had a good visit with her. The next morning when Jim went to see her, he was told that she passed away during the night.

Later when I met a friend, Pam, for a breakfast, she told me about her father. He was not quite himself staying in a hospital. When Pam went to visit him one day, he was alert and they had a very good visit with each other sharing pleasant conversation. Pam thought that he was getting better and had no idea that he was going to die within a day.

Some say that people get better a day or two to spend quality time with their loved ones before they pass away. I don't know how true it is. All I know is that Caesar seemed to be all right when I came home Friday afternoon even though Brendon mentioned Caesar's agitation that started Thursday night. And Caesar was doing well on Saturday when we spent time together. I am wondering, "What did I miss?"

After I arranged Caesar's pictures in a frame, I started to write this little book to keep Caesar's memory alive. After writing about good times with Caesar, I was not able to continue with his nine weeks of illness. After over a month's lapse, I had to tell myself to pull it together to continue. When I started to write about Caesar's first day of illness, I burst into tears. My husband who was working in his office downstairs heard me cry and came up to check on me. I realized that I could not review Caesar's nine weeks illness without tears and would not be able to continue writing unless I was alone to cry without restricting my emotions. Apparently, my grief over Caesar is deeper than I imagined.

So, here I am away from home to be alone for a few days. As I review Caesar's chart to confirm my memory, crying for him and me, I force myself to write about Caesar's illness. Thank goodness for those soft tissues. I stayed inside for a few days, didn't worry about how puffy my face looked, and relived many moments with Caesar until the wee hours of the morning. I know it is not like we have a limited supply of tears. I know that my tears would not dry up just because I shed so many over Caesar during these few days. But it feels good that I can be away from daily chores of taking care of things at home and confine myself in a place to face no one but Caesar's memory. I am grateful to my husband to let me have the time away from home.

While I was going through Caesar's pictures on my laptop, I noticed a function to put one of my favorite pictures as a default screen. How glad I am to see Caesar's happy day on my screen while writing about his days of illness.

Surprisingly, reducing Microsoft Word space to the right side of Caesar's picture does not hinder any writing space. I am grateful to my daughter who bought me this laptop for my birthday last year with a 15" screen and many functions that I didn't think I needed.

When I visit with Caesar every day at home, each day feels like the day after we buried him. There may come the time when I will not shed tears while talking to Caesar. It took over ten years before I was able to talk about my younger brother who died in his mid-twenties. My husband, who never met my brother, knew when my silent tears were for my brother. Lately, he knows when my silent tears are for Caesar.

When I think of my brother, who died young trying to save a friend who was drowning, I feel good about seeing him again later in heaven, but I could not recall any passages in the Bible regarding animals after death. I checked out a book 'Heaven' by Randy Alcorn from the church library to better understand what is ahead for us, hoping to find any remarks about animals. After all, God gave us the ability to love and care.

Oh, Caesar Boy. I long for the day that you will run to me when you hear, "Where is my beautiful Caesar?" If God is willing, anything is possible.

FAREWELL

This is not a farewell to Caesar.

I visit with Caesar, who is laid under his favorite Mesquite tree, every day when I am home, and remember all the fun, good and sad times we had together.

I see Caesar's delightful eyes when he gets a banana from me, feel tickles on my hand when he tries to lick the last lingering flavor, and laugh at his facial expression when he spits out the banana skin that he doesn't think is fit to eat.
I see his face with big eyes acting innocent and his small body dripping water all over after running home from the creek when he heard me calling, "Caesar, where are you?" I see his face enjoying all the attention when I wipe his wet face and body with towels. I just know that he knew that I knew that he would sneak out to the creek again.
I see him walking over to me when I call his name and open the corral gate a couple of inches. He walks ever so slowly so that the other horses would not notice him moving, and sneaks out quietly when I open the gate a couple of feet more.
I see him at the front door patiently waiting for me to come out with his snack. I see him standing next to me eagerly waiting when I reach up to pick mesquite beans.
I see him in the creek pawing and splashing water when we cross the creek. I see him on the road, on the hill, and everywhere we walked and traveled together.

Oh, Caesar. So many memories we shared between you and me. I cannot say farewell to you. You are with me and touch my heart every day. The love and respect that we shared will stay with me. When my memory fades away, you will be remembered through this story forever.
Oh, my Caesar. May you find a better place, may you run in a beautiful grassy field with lots of banana trees, and may you swim in a cool creek for eternity.
Oh, my beautiful Caesar. I long for the day that you will run to me when you hear my voice, "Where is my beautiful Caesar?" If God is willing, anything is possible.

Oh, Caesar Boy. Oh, Caesar Boy. I Miss You So.

Printed in the United States
94242LV00002B